The Merchant of Venice

Illustrated by: Suman S. Roy
Compiled and Edited by: Tapasi De

Contents

1. The Merchant of Venice at a Glance — 3

2. Who's Who in the Play — 5

3. The Merchant of Venice — 8

4. Post-reading Activities — 38

5. About the Author — 40

The Merchant of Venice at a Glance

The Merchant of Venice is one of the most popular plays of Shakespeare which has an interesting plot, memorable characters, tremendously funny and enjoyable situations caused by mistaken identity and disguise. As it is a comedy, it has a happy ending where all the conflicts resolve. A comedy is a piece of literary work which is humourous and evokes laughter.

Shakespearean comedies had certain features due to which his plays seem enjoyable even today.

Glossary
Disguise to give someone a different appearance in order to hide his identity

Themes like young lovers struggling against obstacles which their elders have created, was a common theme. Other themes like mistaken identity, use of multiple plots cleverly intertwined, use of puns, use of stereotype characters and of course a happy ending gave a special touch to all Shakespearean plays.

Glossary
Stereotype a fixed or convention notion about something

Who's Who in the Play

Shylock

Shylock is the central character in the play. He is a Jewish money-lender who gathers money by charging high interest from the Christian merchants.

Portia

Portia is one of the most memorable female characters of Shakespeare. Quick-witted, wealthy and beautiful, Portia is an epitome of virtues.

Glossary
Memorable worth remembering because of being special
Epitome a person or thing that is a perfect example of a particular quality

Antonio

Antonio is the young Christian merchant who is a great friend of Bassanio.

Bassanio

Bassanio is a gentleman of Venice, and a dear friend of Antonio.

Gratiano

Gratiano is a friend of Bassanio who accompanies him to Belmont.

Nerissa

Nerissa is Portia's lady-in-waiting and confidante.

Glossary
Confidante a person with whom one shares a secret or private matter

Jessica

Jessica is Shylock's daughter.

Lorenzo

A friend of Bassanio and Antonio, Lorenzo is the lover of Jessica, Shylock's daughter.

The Merchant of Venice

Long ago, there was a Jew called Shylock, who lived at Venice. He was a money-lender who had gathered an immense fortune by lending money at great interests to Christian merchants. Shylock, being a hard-hearted man, demanded the payment of the money he lent with such severity and cruelty that he was much disliked by all good men. He was particularly hated by Antonio, a young merchant of Venice. Shylock hated Antonio because he used to lend money to people in distress, and would never take any interest for the money he lent! Therefore, there was great enmity between this covetous Jew and the generous merchant Antonio. Whenever Antonio met Shylock on the Rialto (or Exchange), he used to reproach him for his hard dealings, which Shylock would bear with seeming patience quietly. But he secretly planned to take revenge on Antonio someday.

Antonio was the kindest man that ever lived, and was never tired of doing good to others. He was greatly loved by all his fellow-citizens. But the friend who was nearest and dearest to his heart was Bassanio, a noble Venetian. Bassanio had a small inheritance, had nearly exhausted his little fortune by living in an expensive manner. Whenever Bassanio wanted money, Antonio helped him; and it seemed as if they had but one heart and one soul.

One day, Bassanio came to Antonio and said, 'Antonio, I would like to improve my fortune by marrying a wealthy lady whom I love. Her father, who has died recently, has left her with a large estate. When her father was alive, I used to

Glossary
Estate a piece of landed property individually owned
Inheritance a thing that is inherited from the predecessor

visit her house. Many a time, I observed that she looked at me fondly as if she would not refuse me as her suitor. But I do not have the fortune to furnish myself so that I can propose her for marriage. Antonio, you have always helped me whenever I became financially weak. Please lend me your favour one last time by lending me three thousand ducats.'

Antonio at that time had no money with him to lend his friend. But expecting some ships to come home soon laden with merchandise, he said he would go to Shylock, the rich money-lender, and borrow the money upon the credit of those ships.

And so, Antonio and Bassanio went together to Shylock, and Antonio asked the Jew, 'Can you lend me three thousand ducats with any interest that suits you? I will repay you with the merchandise contained in my ships which are in the sea presently, but will arrive home soon.'

Hearing this, Shylock thought within himself, 'If I can once catch him, I will satisfy my grudge which I bear against him. He hates our Jewish community and nation; he lends out money without any

Glossary
Suitor a man who pursues a relationship with a particular woman, with an intention of marriage
Ducats a gold coin formerly used in most European countries
Grudge a persistent feeling of resentment resulting from a past insult

interest. And in front of the merchants he scorns at me and my well-earned bargains, which he calls interest. I can never forgive him!'

When Antonio saw that Shylock was lost in his thoughts he said impatiently, 'Shylock, do you hear? Will you lend the money?' To this question the Jew replied, 'Signor Antonio, on the Rialto many a time you have despised me about the way I lend money to the people and also on the fact that I charge interest. And I have tolerated everything patiently. You have called me an "unbeliever, cutthroat dog", and you have spit upon my garments, and you have neglected me as if I am a dog! Is it possible that a dog should lend three thousand ducats?'

Antonio replied, 'If you will lend me this money, lend it to me not as a friend, but rather lend it to me as to an enemy, that, if I break my promise, you may exact the penalty.'

'Why, look at you,' said Shylock, 'how you are getting agitated! I will be friends with you and have your love. I will forget the insults you have put upon me. I will supply your wants and take no interest for my money.'

This seemingly kind offer greatly surprised Antonio; and then Shylock, still pretending kindness said that he did this in order to gain Antonio's love. He would lend him the three

Glossary
Penalty a punishment given for breaking a law, a rule, or a contract

thousand ducats, and take no interest for his money only for this reason. But Antonio should go with him to a lawyer and there sign a bond that, if he did not repay the money by a certain day, he would allow a pound of flesh to be cut off from any part of his body that Shylock pleased.

'All right,' said Antonio. 'I will sign this bond, and say that there is much kindness in the Jew.'

Bassanio was very disturbed when he heard this. He said, 'Antonio, my brother you should not sign such a bond for me!'

But Antonio insisted saying, 'Dear friend, do not worry for me. Before the day of payment my ships will return laden with many times the value of the money.'

Shylock, hearing this debate amongst the two friends exclaimed, 'O Father Abraham, what suspicious people they are! Their own hard dealings teach them to suspect the thoughts of others. I request you tell me this, Bassanio. If your friend fails in returning the money on the decided day, what should I gain by taking a pound of his

Glossary
Suspicious having distrust of some person or thing

flesh? A pound of man's flesh, taken from a man, is not so valuable, profitable, like the flesh of mutton or beef. I say, to buy his favour I offer this friendship. If he wants he will take it, if not, good bye!'

At last, much against the advice and wishes of Bassanio, Antonio signed the bond, thinking it really was (as the Jew said) merely done in fun.

The rich heiress whom Bassanio wished to marry lived near Venice in a place called Belmont. Her name was Portia, and in her beauty and the presence of her mind she was nothing inferior to that Portia, who was Cato's daughter and the wife of Brutus.

When Bassanio was supplied with money by his friend Antonio, at the risk of his life, Bassanio set out for Belmont with a splendid train and attended by a gentleman called Gratiano. On reaching Belmont, Bassanio proved to be a successful suitor whom Portia readily agreed to marry. Bassanio confessed to Portia that he had no fortune and that his high birth and noble ancestry were all that he could boast of. Portia, who loved him for

Glossary
Heiress a female heir

his worthy qualities and had riches enough not to regard wealth in a husband, answered with a graceful modesty, 'I wish that I was a thousand times more fair, and ten thousand times more rich, to be more worthy of you!'

And then the accomplished Portia prettily dispraised herself and said she was an unlessoned and unschooled girl.

She also said, 'What is mine is yours now! Yesterday, Bassanio, I was the lady of this beautiful mansion, queen of myself, and mistress over these servants. But now this house, these servants and myself are yours, my lord; I give them to you with this ring,' presenting a ring to Bassanio.

Bassanio was so overpowered with gratitude and wonder at the gracious manner in which the rich and noble Portia accepted him that he could not express his joy and reverence. With broken words of love and thankfulness he vowed never to part with it.

Nerissa, Portia's waiting-maid, was present when Portia so gracefully promised to become the obedient wife of Bassanio. And Gratiano, who

Glossary
Dispraised to criticise
Gratitude to be thankful

was also present there desired permission to be married at the same time.

'With all my heart, Gratiano,' said Bassanio.

Gratiano then said that he loved Lady Portia's fair waiting-gentlewoman, Nerissa, and that she had promised to be his wife if her lady married Bassanio. Portia asked Nerissa if this was true. Nerissa replied, 'Madam, it is so, if you approve of it.'

Portia willingly consented. Bassanio pleasantly said, 'Then our wedding-feast shall be much honored by your marriage, Gratiano.'

The happiness of these lovers was sadly interrupted at this moment by the entrance of a messenger, who brought a letter from Antonio containing some fearful news. When Bassanio read Antonio's letter, he looked very pale. And, when she was asked what was the news which so distressed him, he said, 'Oh, sweet Portia, here are a few of the most unpleasant words that ever was written on paper! When I first imparted my love to you, I freely told you that I have spent all the wealth that I had inherited; but I should have told you that I had less than nothing, being in debt.'

Bassanio then told Portia the whole story about

Glossary
Messenger a person who carries a message
Distressed to suffer from extreme anxiety, sorrow, or pain

Antonio's borrowing money from the cruel Shylock and of course about the bond. He also mentioned how Antonio would have to give away a pound of flesh to Shylock if he was unable to repay it on the decided date. And then Bassanio read Antonio's letter, the words of which were:

'Sweet Bassanio, my ships are all lost! And since repaying the Jew seems impossible, I wish to see you at my death. Visit me only if your love for me urges you to, not my letter.'

'My dear Bassanio,' said Portia, 'suspend all business and go; you shall have gold to pay the money twenty times more, before this kind friend shall lose his life.'

Portia then said that she would be married to Bassanio before he set out in order to give him a legal right to her money; and so the same day they were married, and Gratiano was also married to Nerissa. And Bassanio and Gratiano, the instant they were married, set out in great hurry for Venice, where Bassanio found Antonio in prison.

The day of payment had long past. And as

expected, the cruel Shylock would not accept the money which Bassanio offered him, but insisted upon having a pound of Antonio's flesh.

'Signor Bassanio, your friend has knowingly signed the bond which says that I will get a pound of flesh from his body if he fails to repay on the stipulated date. Now what is the use of this money when the date is gone?'

A day was appointed to try this shocking cause before the Duke of Venice, and Bassanio awaited in dreadful suspense the event of the trial.

When Portia had parted with her husband she spoke cheeringly to him and told him to bring his dear friend along with him when he returned. Yet she feared that it would be difficult with Antonio. When she was left alone she began to think if she could by any means be instrumental in saving the life of her dear Bassanio's friend. And despite the promises to be governed by Bassanio's superior wisdom, she resolved to go herself to Venice and speak in Antonio's defense. Not for one moment did she doubt her own abilities in doing so.

Glossary
Duke a nobleman holding the highest hereditary title in the British empire after the Prince

Portia had a relation who was a counsellor in the law. To this gentleman, whose name was Bellario, she wrote, and, stating the case to him, asked his opinion. She also requested him to send the dress worn by a counsellor along with his advice. When the messenger returned, he brought letters from Bellario of advice how to proceed, and also everything necessary for her equipment.

Portia dressed herself and her maid Nerissa in men's apparel. After putting on the robes of a counsellor, she took Nerissa along with her as her clerk. They set out immediately, and arrived at Venice on the very day of the trial. The cause was just going to be heard before the Duke and Senators of Venice in the Senate House, when Portia entered and presented a letter from Bellario. This was the letter in which the learned counsellor wrote to the Duke, saying that he would have come himself to plead for Antonio but he could not due to his sickness. So he requested that the learned young Doctor Balthasar (so he called Portia) might be permitted to plead in his place. This the Duke granted, much wondering at the youthful appearance of the stranger, who was

Glossary
Senators a member of a senate

prettily disguised by her counsellor's robes and her large wig.

And then, began this important trial. Portia looked around her and she saw the merciless Shylock; and she saw Bassanio, but he could not recognise her due to her disguise. He was standing beside Antonio, in an agony of distress and fear of losing his friend. Portia boldly proceeded in the duty she had undertaken. And first of all she addressed Shylock. She clearly said that he had a right by the Venetian law to have the forfeit expressed in the bond but there was a divine quality which needed to be remembered at such situation as this. She spoke so sweetly of the noble quality of MERCY that it would have softened any heart but it had no effect on cruel Shylock's mind. She requested Shylock to remember that as we all pray for mercy, that same prayer should teach us to show mercy also. Hearing all this Shylock said, 'Signor, I only wish to get my 'pound of flesh' as promised in the bond and that is all I can say!'

'Is he not able to pay the money?' asked Portia.

Bassanio then offered the Jew money which was

Glossary
Agony extreme physical or mental pain

many times more than a thousand ducats which Shylock refused still insisting on having a pound of flesh. Bassanio begged the learned young counsellor saying, 'Signor, can you not modify the law a little to save Antonio's life? But Portia gravely answered, 'Laws that once have been established can never be altered!'

Shylock, hearing Portia say that the law cannot be altered, it seemed to him that she was pleading in his favour!

He said excitedly, 'A Daniel is come to judgment! O wise young judge, how I honour you! Though you look so much young, your wits are so matured!'

Portia now told Shylock to let her look at the bond; and when she had read it she said, 'This bond is forfeited, and by this, Shylock may lawfully claim 'a pound of flesh' to be cut off from near Antonio's heart.' Then she said to Shylock, 'Be merciful; take the money and let me tear the bond.'

But the cruel Shylock would show no mercy. He

Glossary
Ducats a gold coin used in most European countries in the olden times.
Forfeited a thing taken away as a penalty for some wrong doing
Merciful to show mercy

said, 'I want nothing but the pound of flesh.'

'Why, then, Antonio,' said Portia, 'you must prepare your bosom for the knife.' And while Shylock was sharpening a long knife with great eagerness to cut off the pound of flesh, Portia said to Antonio, 'Have you anything to say?'

Antonio with a calm resignation replied, 'Nothing at all as I have already prepared for death.' Then he said to Bassanio, 'Give me your hand, Bassanio! Fare you well! Do not be sad that I have fallen into this misfortune for you. Tell your honorable wife how I have loved you!'

Bassanio in the deepest emotion replied, 'Antonio, I am married to a wife who is as dear to me as life. But life itself, my wife, and all the world are above your life. I would lose all, I would sacrifice all to this devil here, to deliver you!'

Portia hearing this, though the kind-hearted lady was not at all offended with her husband for expressing the love he owed to such true a friend as Antonio, yet could not help answering.

'Your wife would not be happy at all to hear this I am sure!'

And then, Gratiano, who loved to copy what his lord did, thought he must make a speech like Bassanio's. And so he said for Nerissa to hear who was writing in her clerk's dress by the side of Portia, 'I have a wife whom I love very much. But

Glossary
Resignation the act of resigning from a job or being passive

I wish she were in heaven so that she could plead for some power to change the cruel temper of this cruel Shylock.'

'It is a blessing that you wish this in her absence, else you would have a lot of noise in your house,' said Nerissa.

Shylock now cried out, impatiently, 'We are wasting our time. I pray pronounce the sentence.'

And now, all present there were full of grief for Antonio. Portia asked if the scales were ready to weigh the flesh and she said to the Jew, 'Shylock, you must have some surgeon or he will bleed to death.'

Shylock, whose whole intention was that Antonio should bleed to death, said, 'It is not written in the bond.'

Portia replied, 'It is not written in the bond, but what of that? It will be good if you did this for charity?'

To this Shylock answered, 'I cannot find it; it is not in the bond.'

Glossary
Surgeon a medical practitioner trained and qualified to practise surgery

'Then,' said Portia, 'a pound of Antonio's flesh is yours. The law allows it and the court awards it. And you may cut this flesh from his breast. The law allows it and the court awards it.'

Again Shylock exclaimed, 'O wise and upright judge! A Daniel is come to judgment!' And then he sharpened his long knife again, and looking eagerly on Antonio, he said, 'Come, prepare!'

'Wait a little, Jew,' said Portia. 'There is something else.

This bond here gives you no drop of blood; the words say, 'a pound of flesh'. If in the cutting off the pound of flesh you shed one drop of Antonio's blood, your lands and goods will be confiscated to the state of Venice by Venetian law.'

Now as it was utterly impossible for Shylock to cut off the 'pound of flesh' without shedding some of Antonio's blood. This wise discovery of Portia that it was the flesh and not the blood that was written in the bond, saved the life of Antonio. Everybody was awestruck at the intelligence and the presence of mind the young counsellor exhibited.

Just then, Gratiano exclaimed, in the words which Shylock had used, 'O wise and upright judge! A Daniel has come to judgment!'

Glossary
Confiscated to seize with authority
Pound a unit of weight

Shylock, finding himself defeated in his cruel intent said, 'Let me have my money and let me go!' He had a disappointed look on his face. And Bassanio, rejoiced beyond measure at Antonio's unexpected deliverance. He cried out, 'Here is the money!'

But Portia stopped him, saying, 'Softly, there is no haste. The Jew shall have nothing but the penalty.

Glossary
Disappointed sad because someone or something has failed to fulfill one's expectations
Deliverance the action of being set free

Therefore prepare, Shylock, to cut off the flesh; but mind you, shed no blood! Moreover, do not cut off more nor less than just a pound. If it is even a bit more or less, if the scale turns but by the weight of a single hair, you will be condemned by the laws of Venice to die, and all your wealth will be forfeited to the state!'

'Give me my money and let me go,' insisted Shylock, nervously.

'I have it ready,' said Bassanio. 'Here it is.'

Shylock was about to take the money, when Portia again stopped him, saying, 'Wait, Jew. I have yet another allegation against you. By the laws of Venice your wealth is forfeited to the state for having conspired against the life of one of its citizens, and your life lies at the mercy of the duke. So down on your knees and ask him to pardon you.'

The duke then said to Shylock, 'I pardon you, your life before you ask for it. Half your wealth belongs to Antonio, the other half comes to the state. This is why our Christian spirit is different from others.'

Glossary
Condemned to disapprove something completely

The generous Antonio then said that he would give up his share of Shylock's wealth if Shylock would sign a deed to pass this wealth to his daughter and her husband after his death. This was because Antonio knew that the Jew had an only daughter who had lately married against his consent a young Christian named Lorenzo, a friend of Antonio. This had angered Shylock so much that he had disinherited her. The Jew agreed to this; and being thus disappointed that he could not take his revenge and he had lost his riches, he said, 'I am ill. Let me go home. Send the deed after me, and I will sign over half my riches to my daughter.'

'Well, you may leave for home,' said the duke, 'and sign it; and if you repent your cruelty, the state will forgive you the fine of the other half of your riches.'

The duke now released Antonio and dismissed the court. He then highly praised the wisdom and ingenuity of the young counsellor and invited him home to dinner. Portia, who meant to return to Belmont before her husband, replied, 'I humbly

Glossary
Disinherited to deprive someone of an inheritance or the right to inherit
Disappointed sad because something or someone has failed to keep up the hope
Ingenuity the characteristic of being original, and inventive

thank your Grace, but I must go away at once!' The duke said he was sorry that he had not leisure to stay and dine with him, and, turning to Antonio, he added, 'Reward this gentleman; for you are much indebted to him.'

After the duke and his senators left the court, Bassanio said to Portia, 'Most worthy gentleman, I and my friend beg you to accept three thousand ducats which was due to the Jew.'

'And we shall stand indebted to you forever,' added Antonio.

But Portia did not accept the money. But upon Bassanio still pressing her to accept some reward, she said, 'Give me your gloves. I will wear them for your sake.'

When Bassanio took off his gloves, she saw the ring which she had given him on his finger. Now it was that ring the crafty lady wanted to get from him to make a merry joke. 'And for your love, I will take this ring from you.'

Bassanio was sadly distressed that the counsellor

Glossary
Leisure free time

should ask him for the only thing he could not part with. In great confusion he replied, 'Signore, I cannot part with this ring because it is my wife's gift and I have vowed never to part with it! Instead of this ring, I can give you the most valuable ring of Venice, after finding it out by proclamation.'

At this, Portia pretended to be offended and left the court saying, 'You teach me, sir, how a beggar should be answered.'

'Dear Bassanio,' said Antonio, 'let him have the ring. Let my love and the great service he has done for me be valued against your wife's displeasure.'

Bassanio, ashamed to appear so ungrateful, yielded, and sent Gratiano after Portia with the ring. And then the 'clerk' Nerissa, who had also given Gratiano a ring, begged his ring, and Gratiano (not choosing to be inferior in generosity by his lord) gave it to her. On their way back, the ladies were amused to recollect the pain that their husbands had gone through while parting with rings. They also discussed how they would tease their husbands for giving away their rings and argue that they had

Glossary
Displeasure a feeling of anger or disapproval
Generosity the virtue of being kind and generous

given them as a present to some woman.

Portia, when she returned, was in that happy temper of mind which stems out of some good action that one has done. Her cheerful spirits enjoyed everything she saw! The moon never seemed to shine so bright before; and when that pleasant moon was hidden behind a cloud, then a light which she saw from her house at Belmont pleased her.

She said to Nerissa, 'That light we see is burning in my hall. How far that little candle throws its beams! By shinning it is doing a good deed in this naughty world.'

In a short while, Portia and Nerissa entered the house, and, dressing themselves in their own clothing, they awaited the arrival of their husbands. Antonio and Bassanio soon entered and Bassanio presented his dear friend to the Lady Portia. The congratulations and welcomings of that lady were hardly over when they saw Nerissa and her husband quarrelling in a corner of the room.

'A quarrel already?' said Portia. 'What is the matter?'

Gratiano replied, 'Lady, it is about an insignificant, gold-washed ring that Nerissa had given me, with words upon it like the poetry on a cutler's knife: 'Love me and leave me not.''

'You swore to me, when I gave it to you, that you would keep it till the hour of death! And now you say that you gave it to the lawyer's clerk. I know you must have given it to some woman.'

Glossary
Insignificant having little importance
Swore past form of swear

'By this hand,' replied Gratiano, 'I gave it to a youth, a boy, no older than you. He was a clerk to the young counsellor who by his wise pleading saved Antonio's life. This chattering boy begged it for a fee, and I could not for my life deny him.'

At this, Portia said, 'You are to blame Gratiano, to part with your wife's first gift. I gave my Lord Bassanio a ring, and I am sure he would not part with it for all the world.'

Gratiano, to excuse himself for his fault, now said, 'My Lord Bassanio gave his ring away to the counsellor first, and then the boy, his clerk, begged for my ring.'

Portia, hearing this, seemed very angry and reproached Bassanio for giving away her ring. She said that she knew some woman had the ring. Bassanio was very unhappy to have so offended his dear lady, and he said with great earnestness, 'No, by my honour, no woman has it, but a young counsellor who asked for the ring, which when I denied him he went away displeased. What could I do, Portia? I was so full of shame for my seeming

Glossary
Counsellor a person who gives guidance on personal or psychological problems
Chattering to talk informally
Reproached to accuse someone of some wrong doing

ingratitude that I was forced to send the ring after him. Pardon me, good lady. Had you been there, I think you would have begged the ring from me to give to the worthy doctor.'

'Ah!' said Antonio, 'I am the unhappy cause of these quarrels.'

Portia told Antonio not to grieve at that, for he was welcome despite everything! And then Antonio said, 'I once did lend my body for Bassanio's sake; and but for him to whom your husband gave the ring was perhaps justified or I should have now been dead. Your lord will never in future break his faith with you.'

'Then you shall be his guarantee,' said Portia. 'Give him this ring and bid him keep it better than the other.'

When Bassanio looked at this ring, he was strangely surprised to find it was the same ring that he had given away! It was only then that Portia told him how she had dressed as the young counsellor and Nerissa was her clerk. Bassanio found to his delight, that it was by

Glossary
Ingratitude ungrateful, thankless
Guarantee a formal written assurance that certain conditions will be fulfilled about a product

the noble courage and wisdom of his wife that Antonio's life was saved! And Portia again welcomed Antonio, and gave him letters which by some chance had fallen into her hands. These letters contained an account of Antonio's ships that were supposed lost, but were safely arriving in the harbour.

So these tragical incidents of this rich merchant's story were all forgotten in the unexpected good fortune which followed. And there was much laughter at the comical adventure of the rings and the husbands not recognizing their own wives! And thus ended this interesting story of love, friendship and intelligence.

Post-reading Activities

Let's see if you remember

1. Name the Jew who used to lend money to the Christian merchants. Describe his nature.

2. Who were the two friends who form the central characters of the play.

3. Which two characters of the play are portrayed exactly opposite to each other in the play? Give reasons.

4. Name the lady whom Bassanio loved. Make a brief character sketch of her.

5. Do you think that it is only for love that Bassanio wanted to marry her or was there any other reason?

6. What was the name of Portia's maid?

7. Why did Antonio want to borrow money from Shylock?

8. What was the condition based on which Shylock agreed to lend money?

9. Could Antonio repay on time? What was the outcome of this?

10. Describe the court scene in which Antonio's life was saved by Portia.

11. What does Portia want as her prize for saving Antonio's life. Why?

12. Can you suggest another title for the story?

About the Author

William Shakespeare was an English poet and playwright, universally acknowledged to be the greatest writer in English language. He is considered to be the world's pre-eminent dramatist also. He lived in the age of Queen Elizabeth I when England enjoyed a time of immense prosperity and stability. He is often called England's national poet and the 'Bard of Avon'.

It is indeed strange that though Shakespeare is recognized as one of literature's greatest influences, very little is actually known about him. Whatever we know about his life comes from the registrar records,

Glossary

Playwright a person who composes plays

court records, wills, marriage certificates and his tombstone.

Early Life

William Shakespeare was born in Stratford-on-Avon, the son of John Shakespeare, a glove maker and dealer in wool. John was a prominent man in Stratford. William's mother was Mary Arden who was the youngest daughter in her family. She inherited much of her father's landowning and farming estate when he died. William was the third child of John and Mary Shakespeare.

Shakespeare probably attended Stratford Grammar School in his childhood. When he was 18, he married Anne Hathaway in 1582. At that time Anne was 26, and already three months pregnant. After sometime his daughter, Susanna, was born. It is generally thought that he must have been in Stratford when Hamnet and Judith, his other two children were born in 1585.

Between the years 1580s and 1592, what Shakespeare did is unknown because no records of his life and works exist of that period. This period of time is often referred to as the 'lost years'. It is possible that he spent this entire period in London after leaving Stratford to escape a charge of deer poaching. Some records say that he was employed at a playhouse 'in a very mean Rank' during this time. Researchers make assumptions that during these 'lost years', Shakespeare might have tended horses for theatergoers or worked as a sailor, a teacher or a coachman. Some think that he might have been a soldier, a law clerk, a theater page, or a moneylender. He could have held several of these jobs or he may have held none of them!

Shakespeare may also have spent the time travelling to far off towns or even to foreign countries. His plays suggest that he visited Italy, for more than a dozen of them including *The Merchant of Venice, Romeo and Juliet, All's Well That Ends Well, Othello, Coriolanus, Julius Caesar, The Two Gentlemen of Verona, The Taming of the Shrew, Titus Andronicus, Much Ado About Nothing*, and *The Winter's Tale*, all have scenes set in Italy.

Career

How Shakespeare first started his career in the theatre no one knows for certain. Whether an acting troupe recruited Shakespeare in his hometown or he was forced on his own to travel to London to begin his career, is not clearly known. In the year 1592 came the first reference to Shakespeare in the world of theatre when Robert Greene an eminent writer of that time mentioned him in his writing. While in London, Shakespeare lived alone in rented accommodations while his wife and children remained in Stratford. Why his family did not move to London with him is unknown.

In 1592, when an epidemic of plague closed the theatres, the versatile Shakespeare wrote sonnets and other poetry until the theatres reopened in 1594. The same year, he joined a newly formed drama group called the 'Lord Chamberlain's Men', serving there as a writer and an actor.

Shakespeare produced most of his well-known works between 1589 and 1613. His early plays were mainly comedies and histories, the literary genre which he raised to the peak of artistic sophistication by the end of the 16th century. He then wrote mainly tragedies until about 1608, including *Hamlet*, *King Lear*, *Othello*, and *Macbeth*, all of which are considered to

Glossary
Versatile able to adapt to many different functions or activities

be the finest works in the English language. In the last years of his career, he wrote tragicomedies, also known as romances, and collaborated with other playwrights.

Shakespeare's works are the greatest representation of art from Elizabethan England. They encompass the economic, social, and educational aspects of life in a nice, neat package. No other art form, including painting, could provide so much information about life in Elizabethan England.

Theatre in Shakespeare's Times

During the age of Shakespeare, all plays which were written had to be approved by the government's censor. This is because plays at that time were considered morally or politically offensive and could be banned. It was considered so very offensive that many a time the playwright would be imprisoned too.

Shakespeare presented his plays at inns, courtyards, royal palaces, private residences, playhouses and the Globe Theatre built in 1599. The playhouses in Shakespeare's time were wooden structures with tiers of seating galleries in the shape of a horseshoe. They could seat two thousand to three thousand people who

Glossary
Imprisoned kept in prison in a captive state

paid two or more pennies. It is believed that at that time the theatre lovers who were wealthy could pay extra to sit on the stage! The main floor, which was surrounded by the galleries, had no roof and no seats. A person could stand and watch the play standing by paying a penny. This area was called a 'pit'. Up to one thousand people could stand and watch performances in this area under a hot sun or dark clouds.

The stage of the Globe Theatre was four to six feet above ground level. There was no curtain that opened or closed at the beginning or at the end of the plays. A wall with two or three doors leading to the dressing rooms of the actors stood at the back of the stage. These rooms collectively were known as the 'tiring house'.

Males played all the characters, even that of women! Actors played gods, ghosts, demons, and other supernatural characters. They could pop up from the underworld through a trap door on the stage or descend down to Earth from heaven on a winch line from the ceiling. The sound of thunder was created off stage, by beating a sheet metal. To demonstrate that an actor had suffered a fencing wound, he simply had to slap his hand against a pouch beneath his shirt to release 'blood' showing his death.

Globe Theatre

Although Shakespeare's plays were performed at different venues during the playwright's career, the Globe Theatre in the Southwark district of London was the place at which his best known plays were first performed. The Globe was built during Shakespeare's early period in 1599 by one of his long-standing associates, Cuthbert Burbage.

The theater that Cuthbert Burbage built had a total capacity between 2,000 and 3,000 spectators. Due to the absence of electric lights, all performances at the Globe were conducted during the day (probably in the mid-afternoon spanning between 2 p.m. and 5 p.m.). As most of the stage of the Globe Theatre was open air and the apparatus for sound system were poor, the actors were compelled to shout their lines, stress their intonations, and engage themselves in exaggerated theatrical gestures. The plays which were staged at the Globe were completely devoid of background scenery although costumes and props were utilized. There was

Glossary
Spectator a person who watches something—a show, a game, or any other event
Apparatus the equipment or machinery needed for a particular activity

no proscenium arch, no curtains, and no stagehands than the actors themselves. Instead, changes of scenes were suggested in the speeches and narrative situations of the plays.

End of Globe Theatre

The original structure of the Globe Theatre existed until June 29, 1613, when its thatched roof was set on fire by a cannon fired during the performance of the play Henry VIII. The Globe burned to ashes and could not be saved. At this time, Shakespeare had almost retired and was at Stratford-on-Avon where he died three years later at the age of fifty-two. The Globe was reconstructed in the year 1614.

Glossary
Proscenium arch it is a kind of an arch which forms a framing on the opening between the stage and the auditorium in some theatres